Managing the Curriculum in Mixed Age Classes

Foundation Stage & Year 1

Original planning work by teachers from a group of small schools in Leicestershire

assisted by Sally Featherstone

This contents of this book are available as a word processed document on CD

Managing the Curriculum in Mixed Age Classes: Foundation Stage & Year 1

ISBN 1 905019 43 2

©Featherstone Education, 2001

Also available in the **Really Good Stuff!** series:

Managing the Curriculum in Mixed Age Classes: Foundation Stage & Key Stage 1

Policy for Teaching and learning, Longlevens Junior School

Policy for Assessment, Recording & Reporting, Longlevens Junior School

Policy & Scheme of Work in PE, Wyvern Primary School

Early Years Audit & Policy Framework

Target Setting Indicators in English, Christ Church & St Peter's Primary School

The following Reception & Year 1 teachers from Leicestershire schools contributed to the planning described in the document:

Pauline Machin & Sarah Hurst, Dove Bank Primary School

Brian Hull, Hemington Primary School

Mary Pole & Debbie Carr, Long Whatton CE Primary School

Rosemary Gould & Maria Lewis Sir John Moore Primary School

Michelle Taylor, Newton Burgoland Primary School

Morag Cooper, St Edward's Primary School

Kerry Muscott, Snarestone Primary School

Steph Brailsford, Stanton Under Bardon Primary School

Consultant: Sally Featherstone

Featherstone Education Ltd
44-46 High Street
Husbands Bosworth
Leicestershire
LE17 6LP

www.featherstone.uk.com

Printed in the United Kingdom on paper produced in the European Union from managed, sustainable forests.

Literacy & Numeracy

These aspects are planned separately, using the literacy and numeracy planners selected by each school, and following the Frameworks.

Literacy

Planning for the literacy lesson follows the word and sentence sections of the Framework, using texts from each theme and additional texts selected by the teacher to reinforce and extend other aspects of literacy.

Foundation Stage children join Year 1 for appropriate parts of the literacy hour. Language and literacy activities for these children are extended through play, role play and other activities linked to the text for the day or week. Activities may be planned for the timetabled literacy lesson or may be available throughout the day. Individual teachers and schools will include this information in their planning.

Children in Year 1 follow the full literacy hour framework, including group work and guided reading. Additional literacy activities for these children may also be built in throughout the day.

The plenary session is either taken at the end of the literacy lesson or at another time during the day planned by the teacher. A combined version of the range section from Reception and Year 1 of the Literacy Framework is included as the English section of each theme in this document, to ensure that texts selected cover the appropriate range.

Numeracy

Numeracy sessions are planned according to the Framework and the guidance for teaching Numeracy in Reception.

Foundation Stage children join Year 1 for appropriate parts of the numeracy lesson. Numeracy activities are then extended through play and practical activities, either in groups at the same time or in activities which children join throughout the day. Individual teachers and schools will include this information in their planning.

As with Literacy, the plenary session is either taken at the end of the numeracy lesson or at another time during the day planned by the teacher. The suggested yearly programme for Reception and Year 1 from the Framework is included as the Mathematics section of each theme in this document to assist with planning.

Other areas of learning & subjects of the curriculum

The following areas and subjects, although they may include material linked with the theme for the half term, are planned weekly to follow the school's schemes, appropriate parts of the Foundation Stage guidance and the National Curriculum Programmes of study.

Creative and other play activities (art, drama, role play, construction, sand, water, etc.)
Physical education (Foundation Stage - Physical Development)
Music (Foundation Stage - Creative Development)
ICT (Foundation Stage - Knowledge and Understanding of the World

Religious education is taught according to the school's schemes and, in Church Aided and Controlled Schools, relevant local guidance.

Multicultural education. Some themes have a major contribution to make to this area of the curriculum. Where multicultural education is not a feature of the theme, teachers will ensure, wherever possible, that RE and other parts of school life include reference to living in a multicultural society. All schools in the group are committed to ensuring that books, stories, pictures, artefacts, play materials and equipment reflect the society in which the children live and will grow up.

LINKS WITH THE QCA SCHEMES OF WORK

At the end of the document, there is an overview of the QCA Schemes and details of where useful information may be found to enhance the themes in the two year cycle.

Time calculations

The teachers who worked on this planning model carried out a **time audit** for their own schools, so that they had an idea of the amount of time available for the thematic part of the curriculum. This is how they did it.

STAGE 1

Work out the total teaching time for a week by:

- calculating the length of the school day
- subtracting registration (am 10mins, pm 5mins)
- subtracting breaks and dinner hour
- subtracting assembly time

Multiply by 5 to get a weekly total

The weekly total for the schools in the group ranged from 18 hours 45 mins to 21 hours 30 mins.

STAGE 2

Subtract the following

Literacy	5 hours
Numeracy	3.75 hours (5 x 3/4 of an hour)
PE	1 – 2 hours (this may be more if you go swimming every week)
Music	30 mins
ICT (skills)	30 mins
RE	30 mins - 1 hour

The amount left ranged from 6 hours 15mins to 7 hours 30 mins.

The planning group decided that the thematic curriculum described in this document would take up the equivalent of between 3 half days and 4 half days, depending on the school. The other parts of the curriculum were to be planned outside the theme, following the Foundation Stage Guidance and frameworks and programmes for National Curriculum subjects.

Suggested two-year cycle of themes

Each series of themes offers opportunities during the year to focus on all areas of learning and experience (Foundation Stage) and all non-core subjects (Key Stage 1). **Science**, as a core subject, appears more frequently. **ICT** is stranded throughout the themes.

All themes offer opportunities for additional creative activities.

Literacy and **numeracy** are planned to link with the themes and to offer a range of texts for Foundation and key stage 1 children.

	First Year	**Second Year**
Autumn 1	*All about me*	*All about us*
	Major – science	Major – PSE
	Minor – history/PSD	Minor - science
Autumn 2	*Toys*	*Let's celebrate!*
	Major – science	Major – creative
	Minor – technol/hi/geog	Minor – science/RE
Spring 1	*Whatever the weather*	*Hot and cold*
	Major – geography	Major – geography
	Minor – science/technology	Minor – PSD/science
Spring 2	*New life*	*Plants*
	Major – science	Major – science
	Minor – PSD/history	Minor – creative
Summer 1	*Minibeasts*	*Splash!*
	Major – science	Major – geography
	Minor – depending on interests	Minor – technology
Summer 2	*Where we live*	*Seaside*
	Major – geography/history	Major – geography/history
	Minor – PSD	Minor – depending on interests

Term by term planning themes with curriculum references

First year of cycle of themes - medium term objectives - two sheets for each theme

EARLY LEARNING GOALS	OBJECTIVES FROM PoS FOR KEY STAGE 1	

EARLY LEARNING GOALS

PERSONAL, SOCIAL & EMOTIONAL DEVELOPMENT
- have a developing awareness of their own needs, views & feelings & be sensitive to the needs, views & feelings of others
- dress & undress independently & manage their own personal hygiene
- consider the consequences of their words & actions for themselves & others

PSD

1a to recognise what they like and dislike, what is fair and unfair, and what is right and wrong
1b to share their opinions on things that matter to them and their views
1c to recognise, name and deal with their feelings in a positive way
1d to think about themselves, learn from their experiences and recognise what they are good at
1e how to set simple goals
2c to recognise choices they can make, and recognise the difference between right and wrong
2d to agree and follow rules for their group and classroom, and understand how rules help them
2e to realise that people and other living things have needs, and that they have responsibilities to meet them
2f that they belong to various groups and communities

LANGUAGE, COMMUNICATION AND LITERACY
- speak clearly & audibly with confidence & control & show awareness of the listener, for example by their use of conventions such as 'please' & 'thank you'
- write their own names

LITERACY Range

Reception	Year 1
• traditional, nursery and modern rhymes, chants, action verses • poetry and stories with predictable structures and patterned language • simple non fiction texts	• stories with familiar settings • stories and rhymes with predictable and repetitive patterns • signs, labels, captions, lists, instructions

MATHEMATICS
- count reliably up to 10 everyday objects

NUMERACY

Reception	Year 1
• Counting • Shape and space • Measures (groups and sets)	• Counting • Money and real life problems • Measures and time • Shape and space • Data

KNOWLEDGE & UNDERSTANDING OF THE WORLD
- find out about, & identify some features of living things and themselves
- find out about past & present events in their own lives and in those of their families
- begin to know about their own cultures & beliefs & those of other people
- find out about their environment

SCIENCE (Sc1 – scientific enquiry to be covered in all themes)

Sc2 1a that animals, including humans, move, feed, grow, use their senses and reproduce
2a to recognise and compare the main external parts of the bodies of humans and other animals
2b that humans and other animals need food and water to stay alive
2c that taking exercise and eating the right types and amounts of food help humans to keep healthy
2g about the senses that enable humans and other animals to be aware of the world around them
4a recognise similarities and differences between themselves and others, and to treat others with sensitivity
Sc4 5c that there are many kinds of sound and sources of sound
5d that sounds travel away from sources, getting fainter as they do so, and that they are heard when they enter the ear

TECHNOLOGY

1c talk about their ideas
1e communicate their ideas using a variety of methods, including drawing and making models
2b explore the sensory qualities of materials
2f follow safe procedures for food safety and hygiene
3a talk about their ideas, saying what they like and dislike

ICT

1a gather information from a variety of sources
3a how to share their ideas by presenting information in a variety of forms
3b to present their completed work effectively
5c talk about the uses of ICT inside and outside school

	1a place events and objects in chronological order 1b use common words and phrases relating to the passing of time 2b identify differences between ways of life at different times 4a how to find out about the past from a range of sources of information 4b to ask and answer questions about the past. 5 select from their knowledge of history and communicate it in a variety of ways 6a changes in their own lives and the way of life of their family or others around them
	GEOGRAPHY 1a ask geographical questions 2e make maps and plans 6a study the locality of the school
	RE
PHYSICAL DEVELOPMENT • show awareness of space, of themselves and others • recognise the importance of keeping healthy & those things which contribute to this • recognise the changes that happen to their bodies when they are active	**PE** 1a explore basic skills, actions and ideas with increasing understanding 2c apply rules and conventions for different activities 4a how important it is to be active 4b to recognise and describe how their bodies feel during different activities 6a use movement imaginatively, responding to stimuli, including music, and performing basic skills 6d express and communicate ideas and feelings 7a travel with, send and receive a ball and other equipment in different ways 8a perform basic skills in travelling, being still, finding space and using it safely, both on the floor and using apparatus 8b develop the range of their skills and actions
	FINE MOTOR SKILLS
CREATIVE DEVELOPMENT • respond in a variety of ways to what they see, hear, smell, touch and feel • express & communicate their ideas, thoughts and feelings by using a widening range of materials, suitable tools, imaginative and role play, movement, designing and making, and a variety of songs and instruments	**ART AND DESIGN** 1a record from first hand observation 2a investigate the possibilities of a range of materials and processes 2b try out tools and techniques and apply these to materials and processes, including drawing 2c represent observations, ideas and feelings, design & make images, & artefacts 3a review what they and others have done and say what they think & feel about it 4a visual and tactile elements, including colour, pattern and texture 5a exploring a range of starting points for practical work 5b working on their own, and collaborating with others, on projects in two and three dimensions and on different scales 5c using a range of materials and processes 5d investigating different kinds of art, craft and design
	MUSIC 1a use their voices expressively by singing songs and speaking chants and rhymes 1b play tuned and untuned instruments 1c rehearse and perform with others 3a explore and express their ideas and feelings about music using movement, dance and expressive and musical language 4a to listen with concentration and to internalise and recall sounds with increasing aural memory 4c how sounds can be made in different ways 5b responding to a range of musical and non-musical starting points 5d a range of live and recorded music from different times and cultures
	DRAMA AND ROLE PLAY a working in role b presenting drama and stories to others c responding to performances

Title: Toys   Term: Autumn 2   Planning year: 1
Major focus: Knowledge & understanding/science   **Minor focus:** Knowledge & understanding/historytechnology

EARLY LEARNING GOALS	OBJECTIVES FROM PoS FOR KEY STAGE 1	
PERSONAL, SOCIAL & EMOTIONAL DEVELOPMENT • be confident to try new activities, initiate ideas & speak in a familiar group • work as part of a group or class, taking turns & sharing fairly, understanding that there need to be agreed values, & codes of behaviour for groups of people, including adults & children, to work together harmoniously	**PSD** a to take part in discussions with one other person and the whole class 2b to take part in a simple debate about topical issues 2d to agree and follow rules for their group and classroom, and understand how rules help them	
LANGUAGE, COMMUNICATION AND LITERACY • use talk to organise, sequence & clarify thinking, ideas, feelings & events • interact with others, negotiating plans & activities & taking turns in conversations	**LITERACY Range** Reception • traditional, nursery and modern rhymes, chants, action verses • poetry and stories with predictable structures and patterned language • simple non fiction texts	Year 1 • stories with familiar settings • stories and rhymes with predictable and repetitive patterns • signs, labels, captions, lists, instructions
MATHEMATICS • use language such as circle, or bigger to describe the shape and size of solids and flat shapes	**NUMERACY** Reception • Counting • Shape and space • Measures (groups and sets)	Year 1 • Counting • Money and real life problems • Measures and time • Shape and space • Data

KNOWLEDGE & UNDERSTANDING OF THE WORLD
• investigate objects & materials by using all of their senses as appropriate
• find out about, & identify some features and objects they observe
• look closely at similarities, differences, patterns & change
• ask questions about why things happen & how things work
• build & construct with a wide range of objects, selecting appropriate resources, & adapting their work where necessary
• select tools & techniques they need to shape, assemble & join the materials they are using
• find out about & identify the uses of technology in their everyday lives & use computers & programmed toys to support their learning
	SCIENCE (Sc1 – scientific enquiry to be covered in all themes)
	Sc3: 1a use their senses to explore and recognise the similarities and differences between materials
	    1b sort objects into groups on the basis of simple material properties
	    1c recognise and name common types of material and recognise that some of them are found naturally
	    1d find out about the uses of a variety of materials & how these are chosen for specific uses on the basis of their simple properties
	Sc4: 2a to find out about, and describe the movement of, familiar things
	    2b that both pushes and pulls are examples of forces
	    2c to recognise that when things speed up, slow down or change direction, there is a cause	

	TECHNOLOGY 1a generate ideas by drawing on their own and other people's experiences 1b develop ideas by shaping materials and putting together components 1c talk about their ideas 1e communicate their ideas using a variety of methods, including drawing and making models 2a select tools, techniques and materials for making their product from a range suggested by the teacher 2c measure, mark out, cut and shape a range of materials 2d assemble, join and combine materials and components 2e use simple finishing techniques to improve the appearance of their product, using a range of equipment 4b how mechanisms can be used in different ways 5a investigating and evaluating a range of familiar products	
	ICT 1a gather information from a variety of sources 2c how to plan and give instructions to make things happen 5b exploring a variety of ICT tools 5c talk about the uses of ICT inside and outside school	

	1a place events and objects in chronological order 1b use common words and phrases relating to the passing of time 3 pupils should be taught to identify different ways in which the past is presented 4a how to find out about the past from a range of sources of information 4b to ask and answer questions about the past. 6b the way of life of people in the more distant past who lived in the local area of elsewhere in Britain 9 pupils should be taught to select from their knowledge of history and communicate it in a variety of ways
	GEOGRAPHY
	RE
PHYSICAL DEVELOPMENT • show awareness of space, of themselves and others • recognise the importance of keeping healthy & those things which contribute to this • recognise the changes that happen to their bodies when they are active	**PE**
	FINE MOTOR SKILLS
CREATIVE DEVELOPMENT • explore colour, texture, shape, form & space in two and three dimensions • express & communicate their ideas, thoughts and feelings by using a widening range of materials, suitable tools, imaginative and role play, movement, designing and making, and a variety of songs and instruments	**ART AND DESIGN** 1a record from first hand observation, experience and imagination, and explore ideas 1b ask and answer questions about the starting points for their work, and develop their ideas 2a investigate the possibilities of a range of materials and processes 2b try out tools and techniques and apply these to materials and processes, including drawing 4b materials and processes used in making art, craft and design 4c differences and similarities in the work of artists, craftspeople and designers in different times 5a exploring a range of starting points for practical work 5b working on their own, and collaborating with others, on projects in two and three dimensions and on different scales 5c using a range of materials and processes 5d investigating different kinds of art, craft and design
	MUSIC
	DRAMA AND ROLE PLAY a working in role b presenting drama and stories to others c responding to performances

Title: Whatever the weather	Term: Spring 1	Planning year: 1

Major focus: Knowledge & understanding/geography   Minor focus: Knowledge & understanding/science/D&T

EARLY LEARNING GOALS	OBJECTIVES FROM PoS FOR KEY STAGE 1

PERSONAL, SOCIAL & EMOTIONAL DEVELOPMENT
- be sensitive to the needs, views & feelings of others

PSD
1b to share their opinions on things that matter to them and their views
1c to recognise, name and deal with their feelings in a positive way

LANGUAGE, COMMUNICATION AND LITERACY
- explore and experiment with sounds, words and texts
- listen with enjoyment and respond to stories, songs, and other music, rhymes and poems and make up their own stories, rhymes and poems

LITERACY Range

Reception	Year 1
• traditional, nursery and modern rhymes, chants, action verses • poetry and stories with predictable structures and patterned language • simple non fiction texts	• traditional and fairy stories and rhymes • familiar, patterned and predictable language • chants, action rhymes, plays • information books and simple dictionaries

MATHEMATICS
- use mathematical ideas and methods to solve practical mathematical problems

NUMERACY

Reception	Year 1	
• Counting • Shape and space • Measures and time • Money and real life	• Counting • Mental calculations • Shape and space • Data	• Money • Measures and time

KNOWLEDGE & UNDERSTANDING OF THE WORLD
- investigate materials by using all of their senses as appropriate
- find out about, & identify some features of events they observe
- look closely at similarities, differences, patterns & change
- ask questions about why things happen & how things work
- build & construct with a wide range of objects, select tools & techniques they need to shape, assemble & join the materials they are using
- observe, find out & identify features in the place they live & the natural world
- begin to know about their own cultures & beliefs & those of other people
- find out about their environment, & talk about those features they like & dislike

SCIENCE (Sc1 – scientific enquiry to be covered in all themes)

Sc1: 2a ask questions and decide how they might find answers to them
2b use first-hand experience and simple information sources to answer questions
2f explore, using the senses of sight, hearing, smell, touch and taste as appropriate, and make and record observations and measurements
2h make simple comparisons (for example, hand span, shoe size) and identify simple patterns or associations
Sc3: 1a use their senses to explore and recognise the similarities and differences between materials
1d find out about the uses of a variety of materials (for example, glass, wood, wool) and how these are chosen for specific uses on the basis of their simple properties
2b explore and describe the way some everyday materials) for example water, chocolate, bread, clay, change when they are heated or cooled

TECHNOLOGY
1b develop ideas by shaping materials and putting together components
1c talk about their ideas
2a select tools, techniques and materials for making their product from a range suggested by the teacher
2d assemble, join and combine materials and components
3a talk about their ideas, saying what they like and dislike
5a investigating and evaluating a range of familiar products
5b focused practical tasks that develop a range of techniques, skills, processes and knowledge
5c design and make assignments using a range of materials, including food, items that can be put together to make products, and textiles

ICT
1a gather information from a variety of sources   1b enter and store information in a variety of forms
2d try things out and explore what happens in real and imaginary instructions

	GEOGRAPHY
	4a make observations about where things are and about other features in the environment
	4b recognise changes in physical and human features (for example, heavy rain flooding fields)
	7b carry out fieldwork investigations outside the classroom

	RE

PHYSICAL DEVELOPMENT	PE
• move with confidence, imagination & in safety	6a use movement imaginatively, responding to stimuli, including music, and performing basic skills

	FINE MOTOR SKILLS

CREATIVE DEVELOPMENT	ART AND DESIGN
• recognise and explore how sounds can be changed, sing simple songs from memory, recognise repeated sounds & sound patterns & match movements to music • respond in a variety of ways to what they see, hear, smell, touch and feel; • use their imagination in art & design, music, dance, imaginative & role play & stories • express & communicate their ideas, thoughts and feelings by using movement, designing and making, and a variety of songs and instruments	1a record from first hand observation, experience and imagination, and explore ideas 2c represent observations, ideas and feelings, and design and make images, and artefacts 5c using a range of materials and processes
	MUSIC
	1a use their voices expressively by singing songs and speaking chants and rhymes 1b play tuned and untuned instruments 2b explore, choose and organise sounds and musical ideas 4c how sounds can be made in different ways and described using given and invented signs and symbols 5b responding to a range of musical and non-musical starting points
	DRAMA AND ROLE PLAY
	a working in role b presenting drama and stories to others c responding to performances

EARLY LEARNING GOALS	OBJECTIVES FROM PoS FOR KEY STAGE 1	
PERSONAL, SOCIAL & EMOTIONAL DEVELOPMENT • continue to be interested, excited & motivated to learn • be confident to try new activities, initiate ideas & speak in a familiar group • maintain attention • have a developing awareness of their own needs, views & feelings & be sensitive to the needs, views & feelings of others • respond to significant experiences, showing a range of feelings when appropriate • work as part of a group or class • select & use activities & resources independently	**PERSONAL, SOCIAL AND HEALTH EDUCATION AND CITIZENSHIP** 1b to share their opinions on things that matter to them and their views 2a to take part in discussions with one other person and the whole class 2e to realise that people and other living things have needs, and that they have responsibilities to meet them	
LANGUAGE, COMMUNICATION AND LITERACY • enjoy listening to and using spoken and written language, and readily turn to it in their play and learning • use language to imagine & recreate roles & experiences • use talk to organise, sequence & clarify thinking, ideas, feelings & events • interact with others • show an understanding of sequence of events, answer questions about where, who, why & how • attempt writing for various purposes, such as lists • write their own names and labels	**LITERACY Range** Reception • traditional, nursery and modern rhymes, chants, action verses • poetry and stories with predictable structures and patterned language • simple non fiction texts	Year 1 • traditional and fairy stories and rhymes • familiar, patterned and predictable language • chants, action rhymes, plays • information books and simple dictionaries
MATHEMATICS • talk about, recognise and recreate simple patterns • use language such as circle, or bigger to describe the shape and size of solids and flat shapes	**NUMERACY** Reception • Counting • Shape and space • Measures and time • Money and real life	Year 1 • Counting • Money • Mental calculations • Shape and space • Measures and time • Data

KNOWLEDGE & UNDERSTANDING OF THE WORLD	SCIENCE (Sc1 – scientific enquiry to be covered in all themes)

• investigate objects & materials by using all of their senses as appropriate
• find out about, & identify some features of living things, objects and events they observe
• look closely at similarities, differences, patterns & change
• ask questions about why things happen
• find out about past & present events in their own lives and in those of their families & other people they know
• observe, find out & identify features in the natural world
	SC1: 2a ask questions and decide how they might find answers to them
	    2b use first-hand experience and simple information sources to answer questions
	    2e follow simple instructions to control the risks to themselves and to others
	    2f explore, using the senses of sight, hearing, smell, touch and taste as appropriate, and make and record observations and measurements
	    2g communicate what happened in a variety of ways., including using ICT
	SC2: 1a the differences between things that are living and things that have never been alive
	    1b that animals, including humans, move, feed, grow, use their senses and reproduce
	    1c to relate life processes to animals and plants found in the local environment
	    2f how to treat animals with care and sensitivity
	    2g that humans and other animals can produce offspring and that these offspring grow into adults

	TECHNOLOGY
	ICT 1a gather information from a variety of sources 3a how to share their ideas by presenting information in a variety of forms 5a working with a range of information to investigate the different ways it can be presented 5b exploring a variety of ICT tools 5c talk about the uses of ICT inside and outside school

	1a place events and objects in chronological order 1b use common words and phrases relating to the passing of time 6a changes in their own lives and the way of life of their family or others around them
	GEOGRAPHY
	RE
PHYSICAL DEVELOPMENT	**PE** 6a use movement imaginatively, responding to stimuli, including music, and performing basic skills 6b change the rhythm, speed, level and direction of their movements 6c create and perform dances using simple movement patterns, including those from different times and cultures 6d express and communicate ideas and feelings
	FINE MOTOR SKILLS
CREATIVE DEVELOPMENT • express & communicate their ideas, thoughts and feelings by using a widening range of materials, suitable tools, imaginative and role play, movement, designing and making, and a variety of songs and instruments	**ART AND DESIGN** 1a record from first hand observation 2a investigate the possibilities of a range of materials and processes 2b try out tools and techniques and apply these to materials and processes, including drawing 2c represent observations, ideas and feelings, design & make images, & artefacts 3a review what they and others have done and say what they think & feel about it 4a visual and tactile elements, including colour, pattern and texture 5a exploring a range of starting points for practical work 5b working on their own, and collaborating with others, on projects in two and three dimensions and on different scales 5c using a range of materials and processes
	MUSIC 1a use their voices expressively by singing songs and speaking chants and rhymes 3a explore and express their ideas and feelings about music using movement, dance and expressive and musical language 4a to listen with concentration and to internalise and recall sounds with increasing aural memory 4c how sounds can be made in different ways 5b responding to a range of musical and non-musical starting points
	DRAMA AND ROLE PLAY a working in role b presenting drama and stories to others c responding to performances

EARLY LEARNING GOALS

OBJECTIVES FROM PoS FOR KEY STAGE 1

PERSONAL, SOCIAL & EMOTIONAL DEVELOPMENT

- continue to be interested, excited & motivated to learn
- be confident to try new activities   • respond to significant experiences
- form good relationships with adults & peers
- understand what is right, what is wrong & why
- dress & undress independently & manage their own personal hygiene
- select & use activities & resources independently
- consider the consequences of their words & actions for themselves & others
- understand that people have different needs, views, cultures & beliefs, which need to be treated with respect
- understand that they can expect others to treat their needs, views, cultures & beliefs with respect

PERSONAL, SOCIAL AND HEALTH EDUCATION AND CITIZENSHIP

1b to share their opinions on things that matter to them and their views
2b to take part in a simple debate about topical issues
2e to realise that people and other living things have needs, and that they have responsibilities to meet them
2g what improves and harms their local, natural and built environments and about some of the ways people look after them

LANGUAGE, COMMUNICATION & LITERACY

- listen with enjoyment and respond to stories, songs, and other music, rhymes and poems and make up their own stories, rhymes and poems
- extend their vocabulary, exploring the meanings & sounds of new words
- show an understanding of elements of stories, such as main character, sequence of events, & how information can be found in non fiction texts, to answer questions about where, who, why & how

LITERACY Range

Reception
- traditional, nursery and modern rhymes, chants, action verses
- poetry and stories with predictable structures and patterned language
- simple non fiction texts
- information texts, recounts of visits and events

Year 1
- fantasy worlds
- poems (themes of poems)

MATHEMATICS

- count reliably up to 10 everyday objects
- use language such as more, less, greater, smaller, heavier, lighter to compare 2 numbers or quantities

NUMERACY

Reception
- Counting
- Shape and space
- Measures (groups and sets)

Year 1
- Counting   • Data
- Money & real life problems
- Shape and space   • Measures and time

KNOWLEDGE & UNDERSTANDING OF THE WORLD

- investigate objects & materials by using all of their senses as appropriate
- find out about, & identify some features of living things, objects and events they observe
- look closely at similarities, differences, patterns & change
- use computers to support their learning
- observe, find out & identify features in the place they live & the natural world
- find out about their environment, & talk about those features they like & dislike

SCIENCE (Sc1 – scientific enquiry to be covered in all themes)

SC1: 2a ask questions and decide how they might find answers to them
2b use first-hand experience and simple information sources to answer questions
2c think about what might happen before deciding what to do
2d recognise when a test or comparison is unfair
2e follow simple instructions to control the risks to themselves and to others
2f explore, using the senses of sight, hearing, smell, touch and taste as appropriate
2g communicate what happened in a variety of ways, including using ICT
2h make simple comparisons and identify simple patterns or associations
2i compare what happened with what they expected would happen. and try to explain it
2j review their work and explain what they did to others

SC2: 1a the differences between things that are living and things that have never been alive
1b that animals, including humans, move, feed, grow, use their senses and reproduce
2f how to treat animals with care and sensitivity
2g that humans and other animals can produce offspring and that these offspring grow into adults
2h about the senses that enable humans and other animals to be aware of the world around them
4b group living things according to observable similarities and differences
5b identify similarities and differences between local environments and ways in which these affect animals found there
5c care for the environment

	1a generate ideas by drawing on their own and other people's experiences 1b develop ideas by shaping materials and putting together components 2c cut and shape a range of materials 2d assemble, join and combine materials and components
	ICT
	HISTORY
	GEOGRAPHY 1c express their own views about people, places and environments 5a recognise changes in the environment 5b recognise how the environment may be improved and sustained
	RE
PHYSICAL DEVELOPMENT • move with confidence, imagination & in safety • move with control and co-ordination • show awareness of space, of themselves and others • handle tools, objects, construction & malleable materials safely and with increasing control	**PE** 6a use movement imaginatively, responding to stimuli, including music, and performing basic skills
	FINE MOTOR SKILLS
CREATIVE DEVELOPMENT • explore colour, texture, shape, form & space in two and three dimensions • sing simple songs from memory • respond in a variety of ways to what they see, hear, smell, touch and feel • use their imagination in art & design, music, dance, imaginative & role play & stories • express & communicate their ideas, thoughts and feelings by using a widening range of materials, suitable tools, imaginative and role play, movement, designing and making, and a variety of songs and instruments	**ART AND DESIGN** 1a record from first hand observation, experience and imagination, and explore ideas 2a investigate the possibilities of a range of materials and processes 2b try out tools and techniques and apply these to materials and processes, including drawing 2c represent observations, ideas and feelings, and design and make images, and artefacts 5a exploring a range of starting points for practical work 5c using a range of materials and processes
	MUSIC
	DRAMA AND ROLE PLAY a working in role b presenting drama and stories to others c responding to performances

EARLY LEARNING GOALS	**OBJECTIVES FROM PoS FOR KEY STAGE 1**	
PERSONAL, SOCIAL & EMOTIONAL DEVELOPMENT • have a developing awareness of their own needs, views & feelings & be sensitive to the needs, views & feelings of others • have a developing respect for their own cultures & beliefs & those of other people • respond to significant experiences, showing a range of feelings when appropriate	**PSD** 1b to share their opinions on things that matter to them and their views 1c to recognise, name and deal with their feelings in a positive way 1d to think about themselves, learn from their experiences and recognise what they are good at	
LANGUAGE, COMMUNICATION AND LITERACY • interact with others, negotiating plans & activities & taking turns in conversations • extend their vocabulary, exploring the meanings & sounds of new words • retell narratives in the correct sequence drawing on the language patterns of stories • speak clearly & audibly with confidence & control & show awareness of the listener, for example by their use of conventions such as 'please' & 'thank you' • know that print carries meaning, and in English, is read from left to right and top to bottom • show an understanding of how information can be found in non fiction texts, to answer questions about where, who, why & how	**LITERACY Range** Reception • traditional, nursery and modern rhymes, chants, action verses • poetry and stories with predictable structures and patterned language • simple non fiction texts • information texts, recounts of visits and events	Year 1 • fantasy worlds • poems (themes of poems)
MATHEMATICS • say and use number names in order in familiar contexts • use language such as circle, or bigger to describe the shape and size of solids and flat shapes • use everyday words to describe position	**NUMERACY** Reception • Counting • Shape and space • Measures (groups and sets)	Year 1 • Counting • Data • Money & real life problems • Shape and space • Measures and time

KNOWLEDGE & UNDERSTANDING OF THE WORLD
• investigate objects & materials by using all of their senses as appropriate
• find out about, & identify some features of living things, objects and events they observe
• build & construct with a wide range of objects, selecting appropriate resources; find out about past & present events in their own lives and in those of their families & other people they know
• observe, find out & identify features in the place they live & the natural world
• find out about their environment, & talk about those features they like & dislike
	SCIENCE (Sc1 – scientific enquiry to be covered in all themes)
	SC1: 2a ask questions and decide how they might find answers to them
	          2b use first-hand experience and simple information sources to answer questions
	SC2: 1c to relate life processes to animals and plants found in the local environment
	          3a to recognise that plants need light and water to grow
	          3b to recognise and name the leaf, flowers, stem and root of flowering plants
	          3c that seeds grow into flowering plants
	          5a find out about the different kinds of plants and animals in the local environment
	          5b identify similarities and differences between local environments and ways in which these affect animals and plants that are found there
	          5c care for the environment
	
	TECHNOLOGY
	2a select tools, techniques and materials for making their product from a range suggested by the teacher
	2c measure, mark out, cut and shape a range of materials
	2d assemble, join and combine materials and components
	2e use simple finishing techniques to improve the appearance of their product, using a range of equipment
	5a investigating and evaluating a range of familiar products	

	1b use common words and phrases relating to the passing of time 2a recognise why people did things, why events happened and what happened as a result 2b identify differences between ways of life at different times 4a how to find out about the past from a range of sources of information 6a changes in their own lives and the way of life of their family or others around them 6b the way of life of people in the more distant past who lived in the local area or elsewhere in Britain
	GEOGRAPHY 1a ask geographical questions 1b observe and record 1c express their own views about people, places and environments 1d communicate in different ways 2a use geographical vocabulary 2b use fieldwork skills 2e make maps and plans 3d recognise how places compare with other places 4a make observations about where things are located and about other features in the environment 6a the locality of the school 7a study at a local scale 7b carry out fieldwork investigations outside the classroom
	RE
PHYSICAL DEVELOPMENT • handle tools, objects, construction & malleable materials safely and with increasing control	**PE**
	FINE MOTOR SKILLS
CREATIVE DEVELOPMENT • use their imagination in art & design, music, dance, imaginative & role play & stories • express & communicate their ideas, thoughts and feelings by using a widening range of materials, suitable tools, imaginative and role play, movement, designing and making, and a variety of songs and instruments	**ART AND DESIGN** 1a record from first hand observation 2b try out tools and techniques and apply these to materials and processes, including drawing 2c represent observations, ideas and feelings, design & make images, & artefacts 3a review what they and others have done and say what they think & feel about it 5a exploring a range of starting points for practical work 5d investigating different kinds of art, craft and design
	MUSIC
	DRAMA AND ROLE PLAY

EARLY LEARNING GOALS

OBJECTIVES FROM PoS FOR KEY STAGE 1

PERSONAL, SOCIAL & EMOTIONAL DEVELOPMENT

- have a developing awareness of their own needs, views & feelings & be sensitive to the needs, views & feelings of others
- have a developing respect for their own cultures & beliefs & those of other people
- respond to significant experiences, showing a range of feelings when appropriate
- form good relationships with adults & peers
- work as part of a group or class, taking turns & sharing fairly, understanding that there need to be agreed values & codes of behaviour for groups of people, including adults & children, to work together harmoniously
- understand what is right, what is wrong & why
- dress & undress independently & manage their own personal hygiene
- select & use activities & resources independently
- consider the consequences of their words & actions for themselves & others
- understand that people have different needs, views, cultures & beliefs, which need to be treated with respect
- understand that they can expect others to treat their needs, views, cultures & beliefs with respect

PSD

1a to recognise what they like and dislike, what is fair and unfair, and what is right and wrong
1c to recognise, name and deal with their feelings in a positive way
1d to think about themselves, learn from their experiences and recognise what they are good at
2a to take part in discussions with one other person and the whole class
2b to take part in a simple debate about topical issues
2c to recognise choices they can make, and recognise the difference between right and wrong
2d to agree and follow rules for their group and classroom, and understand how rules help them
2e to realise that people and other living things have needs, and that they have responsibilities to meet them
2f that they belong to various groups and communities, such as family and school
2h to contribute to the life of the class and school
2l to realise that money comes from different sources an can be used for different purposes (eg. church collections, Sikh tithes)

LANGUAGE, COMMUNICATION AND LITERACY

- interact with others, negotiating plans & activities & taking turns in conversations
- write their own names and labels

LITERACY Range

Reception	Year 1
• traditional, nursery and modern rhymes, chants, action verses	• stories with familiar settings
• poetry and stories with predictable structures and patterned language	• stories and rhymes with predictable and repetitive patterns
• simple non fiction texts	• signs, labels, captions, lists, instructions

MATHEMATICS

- use language such as more, less, greater, smaller, heavier, lighter to compare 2 numbers or quantities

NUMERACY

Reception	Year 1	
• Counting	• Counting	• Data
• Shape and space	• Money & real life problems	
• Measures (groups and sets)	• Shape and space	• Measures and time

KNOWLEDGE & UNDERSTANDING OF THE WORLD

- look closely at similarities, differences
- find out about past & present events in their own lives and in those of their families & other people they know
- begin to know about their own cultures & beliefs & those of other people
- find out about their environment, & talk about those features they like & dislike

SCIENCE (Sc1 – scientific enquiry to be covered in all themes)

Sc2 4a recognise similarities and differences between themselves and others, and to treat others with sensitivity

TECHNOLOGY

ICT

1b enter and store information in a variety of forms
1c retrieve information that has been stored

	6a changes in their own lives and the way of life of their family or others around them
	GEOGRAPHY 5b recognise how the environment may be improved and sustained
	RE
PHYSICAL DEVELOPMENT • move with confidence, imagination & in safety • show awareness of space, of themselves and others	**PE** 2c apply rules and conventions for different activities 6c create and perform dances using simple movement patterns, including those from different times and cultures 7c play simple, competitive net, striking/fielding and invasion-type games that they and others have made, using simple tactics for attacking and defending
	FINE MOTOR SKILLS
CREATIVE DEVELOPMENT • explore colour, texture, shape, form & space in two and three dimensions • express & communicate their ideas, thoughts and feelings	**ART AND DESIGN** 5b working on their own, and collaborating with others, on projects in two and three dimensions and on different scales
	MUSIC 5c pupils working on their own, in groups of different sizes and as a class 5d a range of live and recorded music from different times and cultures
	DRAMA AND ROLE PLAY a working in role b presenting drama and stories to others c responding to performances

EARLY LEARNING GOALS	OBJECTIVES FROM PoS FOR KEY STAGE 1	
PERSONAL, SOCIAL & EMOTIONAL DEVELOPMENT • have a developing respect for their own cultures & beliefs & those of other people • understand that people have different needs, views, cultures & beliefs, which need to be treated with respect • understand that they can expect others to treat their needs, views, cultures & beliefs with respect	**PSD** 2a to take part in discussions with one other person and the whole class 2b to take part in a simple debate about topical issues 2f that they belong to various groups and communities, such as family and school 2l to realise that money comes from different sources an can be used for different purposes	
LANGUAGE, COMMUNICATION AND LITERACY • listen with enjoyment and respond to stories, songs, and other music, rhymes and poems and make up their own stories, rhymes and poems • extend their vocabulary, exploring the meanings & sounds of new words	**LITERACY Range** Reception • traditional, nursery and modern rhymes, chants, action verses • poetry and stories with predictable structures and patterned language • simple non fiction texts	Year 1 • stories with familiar settings • stories and rhymes with predictable and repetitive patterns • signs, labels, captions, lists, instructions
MATHEMATICS	**NUMERACY** Reception • Counting • Shape and space • Measures	Year 1 • Counting • Money & real life problems • Shape and space • Measures and time
KNOWLEDGE & UNDERSTANDING OF THE WORLD • investigate objects & materials by using all of their senses as appropriate • look closely at similarities, differences, patterns & change • find out about past & present events in their own lives and in those of their families & other people they know • begin to know about their own cultures & beliefs & those of other people • find out about their environment, & talk about those features they like & dislike	**SCIENCE (Sc1 – scientific enquiry to be covered in all themes)** SC1: 2a ask questions and decide how they might find answers to them 2b use first-hand experience and simple information sources to answer questions 2c think about what might happen before deciding what to do 2d recognise when a test or comparison is unfair 2e follow simple instructions to control the risks to themselves and to others 2f explore, using the senses of sight, hearing, smell, touch and taste as appropriate, and make and record observations and measurements 2g communicate what happened in a variety of ways 2h make simple comparisons and identify simple patterns or associations 2i compare what happened with what they expected would happen, and try to explain it. Drawing on their knowledge and understanding 2j review their work and explain what they did to others SC4: 1a about everyday appliances that use electricity 1b about simple series circuits involving batteries, wires, bulbs and other components 1c how a switch can be used to break a circuit 3a to identify different light sources, including the Sun 3b that darkness is the absence of light	
	TECHNOLOGY 1a generate ideas by drawing on their own and other people's experiences 1b develop ideas by shaping materials and putting together components 1c talk about their ideas 1d plan by suggesting what to do next as their ideas develop 1e communicate their ideas using a variety of methods, including drawing and making models 2a select tools, techniques and materials for making their product from a range suggested by the teacher 2b explore the sensory qualities of materials 2c measure, mark out, cut and shape a range of materials 2d assemble, join and combine materials and components 2e use simple finishing techniques to improve the appearance of their product, using a range of equipment	

		HISTORY
		6b the way of life of people in the more distant past
		GEOGRAPHY
		3e recognise how places are linked to other places in the world
		RE
PHYSICAL DEVELOPMENT		**PE**
		3a describe what they have done
		3b observe, describe and copy what others have done
		3c use what they have learnt to improve the quality and control of their work
		6a use movement imaginatively, responding to stimuli, including music, and performing basic skills
		6b change the rhythm, speed, level and direction of their movements
		6c create and perform dances using simple movement patterns, including those from different times and cultures
		6d express and communicate ideas and feelings
		FINE MOTOR SKILLS
		ART AND DESIGN
		1a record from first hand observation, experience and imagination, and explore ideas
		1b ask and answer questions about the starting points for their work, and develop their ideas
		2a investigate the possibilities of a range of materials and processes
CREATIVE DEVELOPMENT		2b try out tools and techniques and apply these to materials and processes, including drawing
• explore colour, texture, shape, form & space in two and three dimensions		2c represent observations, ideas and feelings, and design and make images, and artefacts
• respond in a variety of ways to what they see, hear, smell, touch and feel		3a review what they and others have done and say what they think and feel about it
• use their imagination in art & design, music, dance, imaginative & role play & stories		4a visual and tactile elements, including colour, pattern and texture, line and tone, shape, form and space
• express & communicate their ideas, thoughts and feelings by using a widening range of materials, suitable tools, imaginative and role play, movement, designing and making, and a variety of songs and instruments		4b materials and processes used in making art, craft and design
		5a exploring a range of starting points for practical work
		5b working on their own, and collaborating with others, on projects in two and three dimensions and on different scales
		5c using a range of materials and processes
		5d investigating different kinds of art, craft and design
		MUSIC
		1a use their voices expressively by singing songs and speaking chants and rhymes
		1b play tuned and untuned instruments
		1c rehearse and perform with others
		2a create musical patterns
		2b explore, choose and organise sounds and musical ideas
		3a explore and express their ideas and feelings about music using movement, dance and expressive & musical language
		3b make improvements to their own work
		4d how music is used for particular purposes
		5a a range of musical activities that integrate performing, composing and appraising
		5b responding to a range of musical and non-musical starting points
		5c pupils working on their own, in groups of different sizes and as a class
		5d a range of live and recorded music from different times and cultures
		DRAMA AND ROLE PLAY
		a working in role
		b presenting drama and stories to others
		c responding to performances

EARLY LEARNING GOALS	OBJECTIVES FROM PoS FOR KEY STAGE 1	
PERSONAL, SOCIAL & EMOTIONAL DEVELOPMENT • continue to be interested, excited & motivated to learn • have a developing respect for their own cultures & beliefs & those of other people • understand that people have different needs, views, cultures & beliefs, which need to be treated with respect • understand that they can expect others to treat their needs, views, cultures & beliefs with respect	**PSD** 2a to take part in discussions with one other person and the whole class 2h to contribute to the life of the class and school	
LANGUAGE, COMMUNICATION AND LITERACY • enjoy listening to and using spoken and written language, and readily turn to it in their play and learning • use language to imagine & recreate roles & experiences • interact with others, negotiating plans & activities & taking turns in conversations	**LITERACY Range** Reception • traditional, nursery and modern rhymes, chants, action verses • poetry and stories with predictable structures and patterned language • simple non fiction texts	Year 1 • traditional and fairy stories and rhymes • familiar, patterned and predictable language • chants, action rhymes, plays • information books and simple dictionaries
MATHEMATICS	**NUMERACY** Reception • Counting • Shape and space • Measures and time • Money and real life	Year 1 • Counting • Money • Mental calculations • Shape and space • Measures and time • Data

KNOWLEDGE & UNDERSTANDING OF THE WORLD
• investigate objects & materials by using all of their senses as appropriate
• look closely at similarities, differences, patterns & change
• observe, find out & identify features in the place they live & the natural world
• begin to know about their own cultures & beliefs & those of other people
• find out about their environment, & talk about those features they like & dislike
	SCIENCE (Sc1 – scientific enquiry to be covered in all themes)
	SC1: 2a ask questions and decide how they might find answers to them
	     2b use first-hand experience and simple information sources to answer questions
	     2c think about what might happen before deciding what to do
	     2d recognise when a test or comparison is unfair
	     2e follow simple instructions to control the risks to themselves and to others
	     2f explore, using the senses of sight, hearing, smell, touch and taste as appropriate, and make and record observations and measurements
	     2g communicate what happened in a variety of ways
	     2h make simple comparisons and identify simple patterns or associations
	     2i compare what happened with what they expected would happen, and try to explain it. Drawing on their knowledge and understanding
	     2j review their work and explain what they did to others
	SC3: 1a use their senses to explore and recognise the similarities and differences between materials
	     2b explore and describe the way some everyday materials change when they are heated or cooled	

	TECHNOLOGY 2f follow safe procedures for food safety and hygiene 5c design and make assignments using a range of materials, including food, items that can be put together to make products, and textiles	
	ICT 1a gather information from a variety of sources 5c talk about the uses of ICT inside and outside school 2a use geographical vocabulary 2c use globes, maps and plans at a range of scales 2d use secondary sources of information	

	GEOGRAPHY 1a ask geographical questions 1b observe and record 1c express their own views about people, places and environments 1d communicate in different ways 3a identify and describe what places are like 3d recognise how places compare with other places 3e recognise how places are linked to other places in the world 6b a locality either in the United Kingdom or overseas that has physical and/or human features that contrast with those in the locality of the school
	RE
PHYSICAL DEVELOPMENT • recognise the importance of keeping healthy & those things which contribute to this • recognise the changes that happen to their bodies when they are active	**PE** 3a describe what they have done 3b observe, describe and copy what others have done 4a how important it is to be active 4b to recognise and describe how their bodies feel during different activities 6a use movement imaginatively, responding to stimuli, including music, and performing basic skills 6b change the rhythm, speed, level and direction of their movements 6c create and perform dances using simple movement patterns, including those from different times and cultures 6d express and communicate ideas and feelings
	FINE MOTOR SKILLS
CREATIVE DEVELOPMENT • explore colour, texture, shape, form & space in two and three dimensions • respond in a variety of ways to what they see, hear, smell, touch and feel	**ART AND DESIGN** 1a record from first hand observation 2a investigate the possibilities of a range of materials and processes 2b try out tools and techniques and apply these to materials and processes, including drawing 2c represent observations, ideas and feelings, design & make images, & artefacts 3a review what they and others have done and say what they think & feel about it 4a visual and tactile elements, including colour, pattern and texture 5a exploring a range of starting points for practical work 5b working on their own, and collaborating with others, on projects in two and three dimensions and on different scales 5c using a range of materials and processes 5d investigating different kinds of art, craft and design
	MUSIC 1a use their voices expressively by singing songs and speaking chants and rhymes 2b explore, choose and organise sounds and musical ideas 5b responding to a range of musical and non-musical starting points 5d a range of live and recorded music from different times and cultures
	DRAMA AND ROLE PLAY a working in role b presenting drama and stories to others c responding to performances

EARLY LEARNING GOALS	OBJECTIVES FROM PoS FOR KEY STAGE 1	
PERSONAL, SOCIAL & EMOTIONAL DEVELOPMENT • continue to be interested, excited & motivated to learn • be confident to try new activities, initiate ideas & speak in a familiar group; • maintain attention, concentration & sit quietly when appropriate • work as part of a group or class • select & use activities & resources independently	**PSD** 1a to recognise what they like and dislike, what is fair and unfair, and what is right and wrong 1c to recognise, name and deal with their feelings in a positive way 2e to realise that people and other living things have needs, and that they have responsibilities to meet them 2g what improves and harms their local, natural and built environments and about some of the ways people look after them	
LANGUAGE, COMMUNICATION AND LITERACY • enjoy listening to and using spoken and written language, and readily turn to it in their play and learning • use talk to organise, sequence & clarify thinking, ideas, feelings & events; • interact with others, negotiating plans & activities & taking turns in conversations • show an understanding of sequence of events & how information can be found in non fiction texts, to answer questions about where, who, why & how • attempt writing for various purposes • write their own labels	**LITERACY Range** Reception • traditional, nursery and modern rhymes, chants, action verses • poetry and stories with predictable structures and patterned language • simple non fiction texts	Year 1 • traditional and fairy stories and rhymes • familiar, patterned and predictable language • chants, action rhymes, plays • information books and simple dictionaries
MATHEMATICS • count reliably up to 10 everyday objects • use language such as more, less, greater, smaller, heavier, lighter to compare 2 numbers or quantities • talk about, recognise and recreate simple patterns • use language such as circle, or bigger to describe the shape and size of solids and flat shapes • use everyday words to describe position	**NUMERACY** Reception • counting • shape and space • measures (groups and sets)	Year 1 • Counting • Money • Mental calculations • Shape and space • Measures and time • Data
KNOWLEDGE & UNDERSTANDING OF THE WORLD • investigate objects & materials by using all of their senses as appropriate • find out about, & identify some features of living things, objects and events they observe • look closely at similarities, differences, patterns & change • ask questions about why things happen & how things work • observe, find out & identify features in the place they live & the natural world • find out about their environment, & talk about those features they like & dislike	**SCIENCE (Sc1 – scientific enquiry to be covered in all themes)** SC1: 2a ask questions and decide how they might find answers to them 2b use first-hand experience and simple information sources to answer questions 2c think about what might happen before deciding what to do 2d recognise when a test or comparison is unfair 2e follow simple instructions to control the risks to themselves and to others 2f explore, using the senses of sight, hearing, smell, touch and taste as appropriate 2g communicate what happened in a variety of ways 2h make simple comparisons and identify simple patterns or associations 2i compare what happened with what they expected would happen, and try to explain it. 2j review their work and explain what they did to others SC2: 1a the differences between things that are living and things that have never been alive 1c to relate life processes to plants found in the local environment 3a to recognise that plants need light and water to grow 3b to recognise and name the leaf, flowers, stem and root of flowering plants 3c that seeds grow into flowering plants 4b group living things according to observable similarities and differences 5a find out about the different kinds of plants and animals in the local environment	
	TECHNOLOGY 1e communicate their ideas using a variety of methods, including drawing and making models 2b explore the sensory qualities of materials 4a about the working characteristics of materials	

	1a gather information from a variety of sources 2a to use text, tables, images and sound to develop their ideas 3a how to share their ideas by presenting information in a variety of forms 3b to present their completed work effectively 5a working with a range of information to investigate the different ways it can be presented
	HISTORY
	GEOGRAPHY 1a ask geographical questions 1d communicate in different ways 4a make observations about where things are located and about other features in the environment 6a the locality of the school
	RE
PHYSICAL DEVELOPMENT • handle tools, objects, construction & malleable materials safely and with increasing control	**PE** 1b remember and repeat simple skills and actions with increasing control and co-ordination 6a use movement imaginatively, responding to stimuli, including music, and performing basic skills
	FINE MOTOR SKILLS
CREATIVE DEVELOPMENT • explore colour, texture, shape, form & space in two and three dimensions • respond in a variety of ways to what they see, hear, smell, touch and feel • use their imagination in art & design, music, dance, imaginative & role play & stories • express & communicate their ideas, thoughts and feelings by using a widening range of materials, suitable tools, imaginative and role play, movement, designing and making, and a variety of songs and instruments	**ART AND DESIGN** 1a record from first hand observation, experience and imagination, and explore ideas 2a investigate the possibilities of a range of materials and processes 2c represent observations, ideas and feelings, and design and make images, and artefacts 4c differences and similarities in the work of artists, craftspeople and designers in different times and cultures 5b pupils working on their own, and collaborating with others, on projects in two and three dimensions and on different scales 5c using a range of materials and processes
	MUSIC 3a explore and express their ideas and feelings about music using movement, dance and expressive and musical language
	DRAMA AND ROLE PLAY a working in role b presenting drama and stories to others c responding to performances

EARLY LEARNING GOALS	OBJECTIVES FROM PoS FOR KEY STAGE 1	

PERSONAL, SOCIAL & EMOTIONAL DEVELOPMENT

- have a developing awareness of their own needs, views & feelings & be sensitive to the needs, views & feelings of others
- manage their own personal hygiene

PSD

2d to agree and follow rules for their group and classroom, and understand how rules help them

2e to realise that people and other living things have needs, and that they have responsibilities to meet them

---

LANGUAGE, COMMUNICATION AND LITERACY

- enjoy listening to and using spoken and written language, and readily turn to it in their play and learning
- explore and experiment with sounds, words and texts
- listen with enjoyment and respond to stories, songs, and other music, rhymes and poems and make up their own stories, rhymes and poems
- extend their vocabulary, exploring the meanings & sounds of new words

LITERACY Range

Reception
- traditional, nursery and modern rhymes, chants, action verses
- poetry and stories with predictable structures and patterned language
- simple non fiction texts

Year 1
- fantasy worlds
- poems (themes of poems)
- information texts, recounts of visits and events

MATHEMATICS

- use language such as more, less, greater, smaller, heavier, lighter to compare 2 numbers or quantities

NUMERACY

Reception
- counting
- shape and space
- measures (groups and sets)

Year 1
- Counting
- Money   • Mental calculations
- Shape and space   • Measures and time
- Data

KNOWLEDGE & UNDERSTANDING OF THE WORLD

- investigate objects & materials by using all of their senses as appropriate
- find out about, & identify some features of living things, objects and events they observe
- look closely at similarities, differences, patterns & change
- ask questions about why things happen & how things work
- build & construct with a wide range of objects, selecting appropriate resources, & adapting their work where necessary
- observe, find out & identify features in the place they live & the natural world
- begin to know about their own cultures & beliefs & those of other people
- find out about their environment, & talk about those features they like & dislike

SCIENCE (Sc1 – scientific enquiry to be covered in all themes)

SC1: 2a ask questions and decide how they might find answers to them

2b use first-hand experience and simple information sources to answer questions

2c think about what might happen before deciding what to do

2d recognise when a test or comparison is unfair

2e follow simple instructions to control the risks to themselves and to others

2f explore, using the senses of sight, hearing, smell, touch and taste as appropriate, and make and record observations and measurements

2g communicate what happened in a variety of ways

2h make simple comparisons and identify simple patterns or associations

2i compare what happened with what they expected would happen, and try to explain it.

2j review their work and explain what they did to others

SC2: 2c that taking exercise and eating the right types and amounts of food help humans to keep healthy

3a to recognise that plants need light and water to grow

SC3: 1b sort objects into groups on the basis of simple material properties

2b explore and describe the way some everyday materials change when they are heated or cooled

TECHNOLOGY

ICT

1a gather information from a variety of sources

3a how to share their ideas by presenting information in a variety of forms

5a working with a range of information to investigate the different ways it can be presented

5c talk about the uses of ICT inside and outside school

	GEOGRAPHY 1a ask geographical questions 1b observe and record 1c express their own views about people, places and environments 1d communicate in different ways 2a use geographical vocabulary 2b use fieldwork skills 2c use globes, maps and plans at a range of scales 2d use secondary sources of information 3a identify and describe what places are like 3b identify and describe what places are 4a make observations about features in the environment 4b recognise changes in physical and human features 6a the locality of the school 7a study at a local scale 7b carry out fieldwork investigations outside the classroom
PHYSICAL DEVELOPMENT • recognise the importance of keeping healthy & those things which contribute to this	
	RE
	PE
	FINE MOTOR SKILLS
CREATIVE DEVELOPMENT • recognise and explore how sounds can be changed, sing simple songs from memory, recognise repeated sounds & sound patterns & match movements to music • respond in a variety of ways to what they see, hear, smell, touch and feel • use their imagination in art & design, music, dance, imaginative & role play & stories	**ART AND DESIGN** 2c represent observations, ideas and feelings, design & make images, & artefacts 4a visual and tactile elements, including colour, pattern and texture
	MUSIC 1b play tuned and untuned instruments 2a create musical patterns 3a explore and express their ideas and feelings about music using movement, dance and expressive and musical language 4a to listen with concentration and to internalise and recall sounds with increasing aural memory 4c how sounds can be made in different ways and described using given and invented signs and symbols 5b responding to a range of musical and non-musical starting points
	DRAMA AND ROLE PLAY a working in role b presenting drama and stories to others c responding to performances

EARLY LEARNING GOALS	OBJECTIVES FROM PoS FOR KEY STAGE 1	
PERSONAL, SOCIAL & EMOTIONAL DEVELOPMENT • respond to significant experiences, showing a range of feelings when appropriate	**PSD** 1a to recognise what they like and dislike, what is fair and unfair, and what is right and wrong 2a to take part in discussions with one other person and the whole class 2e to realise that people and other living things have needs, and that they have responsibilities to meet them	
LANGUAGE, COMMUNICATION AND LITERACY • listen with enjoyment and respond to stories, songs, and other music, rhymes and poems and make up their own stories, rhymes and poems • use language to imagine & recreate roles & experiences • attempt writing for various purposes, using features of different forms such as lists, stories, instructions	**LITERACY Range** Reception • traditional, nursery and modern rhymes, chants, action verses • poetry and stories with predictable structures and patterned language • simple non fiction texts • information textx, recountds of visits and events	Year 1 • fantasy worlds • poems (themes of poems)
MATHEMATICS • count reliably up to 10 everyday objects	**NUMERACY** Reception • counting • shape and space • measures	Year 1 • Counting • Money • Mental calculations • Shape and space • Measures and time • Data

KNOWLEDGE & UNDERSTANDING OF THE WORLD
• look closely at similarities, differences, patterns & change
• ask questions about why things happen & how things work
• find out about past & present events in their own lives and in those of their families & other people they know
• observe, find out & identify features in the place they live & the natural world
• find out about their environment, & talk about those features they like & dislike
	SCIENCE (Sc1 – scientific enquiry to be covered in all themes)
	SC1: 2a ask questions and decide how they might find answers to them
	      2f explore, using the senses of sight, hearing, smell, touch and taste as appropriate, and make and record observations and measurements
	      2h make simple comparisons and identify simple patterns or associations
	SC2: 5b identify similarities & differences between local environments & ways in which these affect animals & plants that are found there	

	TECHNOLOGY 1e communicate their ideas using a variety of methods, including drawing and making models 2a select tools, techniques and materials for making their product from a range suggested by the teacher 2d assemble, join and combine materials and components 2f follow safe procedures for food safety and hygiene 3a talk about their ideas, saying what they like and dislike 5c design and make assignments using a range of materials, including food, items that can be put together to make products, and textiles	
	ICT 1a gather information from a variety of sources 3a how to share their ideas by presenting information in a variety of forms 5b exploring a variety of ICT tools	

	2a recognise why people did things, why events happened and what happened as a result 2b identify differences between ways of life at different times 4a how to find out about the past from a range of sources of information 6a changes in their own lives and the way of life of their family or others around them
	GEOGRAPHY 1a ask geographical questions 1c express their own views about people, places and environments 2a use geographical vocabulary 2d use secondary sources of information 3a identify and describe what places are like 3d recognise how places compare with other places 6b a locality either in the United Kingdom or overseas that has physical and/or human features that contrast with those in the locality of the school
	RE
PHYSICAL DEVELOPMENT	**PE** 4a how important it is to be active 6a use movement imaginatively, responding to stimuli, including music, and performing basic skills 6b change the rhythm, speed, level and direction of their movements 7a travel with, send and receive a ball and other equipment in different ways 7c play simple, competitive net, striking/fielding and invasion-type games that they and others have made, using simple tactics for attacking and defending 8b develop the range of their skills and actions
	FINE MOTOR SKILLS
CREATIVE DEVELOPMENT • explore colour, texture, shape, form & space in two and three dimensions • use their imagination in art & design, music, dance, imaginative & role play & stories • express & communicate their ideas, thoughts and feelings by using a widening range of materials, suitable tools, imaginative and role play, movement, designing and making, and a variety of songs and instruments	**ART AND DESIGN** 2a investigate the possibilities of a range of materials and processes 4a visual and tactile elements, including colour, pattern and texture, line and tone, shape, form and space 5a exploring a range of starting points for practical work
	MUSIC 1a use their voices expressively by singing songs and speaking chants and rhymes 3a explore and express their ideas and feelings about music using movement, dance and expressive and musical language 5d a range of live and recorded music from different times and cultures
	DRAMA AND ROLE PLAY a working in role b presenting drama and stories to others c responding to performances

Links with the QCA schemes of work

An overview of the QCA Schemes of work for non-core subjects, and where useful information may be found to enhance the themes in the two year cycle.

	First Year		Second Year	
	All about me		**All about us**	
	Major: science Minor: history/PSD		Major: PSE Minor: science	
Autumn 1	Science 1A, 1F History 2 Geog 1 D&T 1C	ICT 1A, 1B, 1C Music 2, 6 Art 1A, 2A PE 1	Science 1A, History 2, 17 Geog 1, 2 D&T	ICT Music 4 Art 1A, 2A PE Dance 1, Games 1, Gym1
	Toys		**Let's celebrate**	
	Major: science Minor: tech/hi/geog		Major: creative Minor: science/RE	
Autumn 2	Science 1C History 1 Geog D&T1A, 2A, 2B	ICT 1D, 1E, 1F, 2C, 2D Music Art 1B PE	Science 1D, 2F History 2 Geog D&T1C	ICT Music 1, 2, 6 Art 1C PE 1, 2
	Whatever the weather		**Hot and cold**	
	Major: geography Minor: science/tech		Major: geography Minor: PSD/science	
Spring 1	Science 1C History Geog 5 D&T	ICT 1C, 1E Music 1, 2, 7 Art 1B PE Dance 1	Science 2D History Geog 3, 5 D&T 1C	ICT 1C Music 1 Art 1C PE Dance 1, 2

	First Year		Second Year	
	New life		**Plants**	
	Major: science Minor: PSD/history		Major: science Minor: creative	
Spring 2	Science 1A, 1B, 2A, 2B History Geog D&T	ICT 1C Music 1 Art PE Dance 1, 2	Science 1B History Geog D&T 1A	ICT 1A, 1B Music Art 1C, 2B PE
	Minibeasts		**Splash!**	
	Major: science Minor:		Major: geography Minor: PSD	
Summer 1	Science 1A, 2B History Geog D&T 1A, 1D, 2B	ICT 1C, 1D, 1E Music Art 2B PE	Science 1A, History Geog D&T	ICT Music Art PE
	Our village		**Seaside**	
	Major: geog/hi Minor: technology		Major: geog/hi Minor:	
Summer 2	Science 1A, History Geog D&T	ICT Music Art PE	Science History 3 Geog 4, 5 D&T1B	ICT 1c, 2b Music 1 Art 2A, 2B, 1C PE Dance 1, Games 1

The full text of this document is also available in Microsoft Word format on CD, for users to edit to meet their own needs.

Please contact the publishers to order.